美良藏書

I Love You

© By Massada Press Ltd. Jerusalem

Library of Congress Cataloging-in-Publication Data

Rennert, Meggie.
I love you.

Summary: Describes the many ways to say "I love you"
to animals, relatives, friends, and the world.
(1. Love-Fiction) I. Frankel, alona, ill.
II. Title.
PZ7. R2915Ial   1987   (E)   87-1845
ISBN 0-915361-71-X

Adama Books, 306 West 38 Street, New York, N. Y. 10018

Printed in Israel

I LOVE YOU

By Maggie Rennert
Illustrated by Alona Frankel

ADAMA BOOKS, NEW YORK

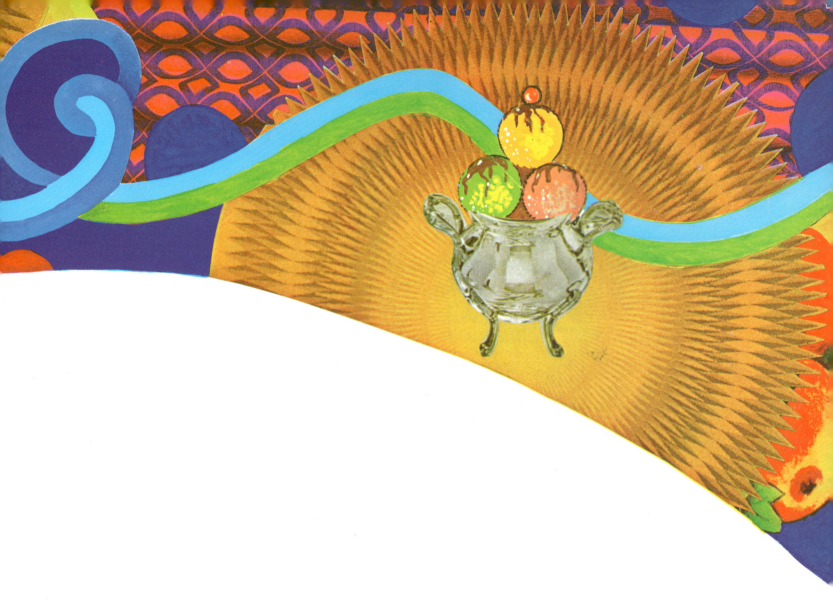

Every morning, you know what I say
to the world out there, when I start a new day?
I love you, everybody.

In fact, I love lots of things — days old and new,
and good things to eat, and nice people too.

One kind of loving that's easy to do,
is love back whomever quite clearly loves you...

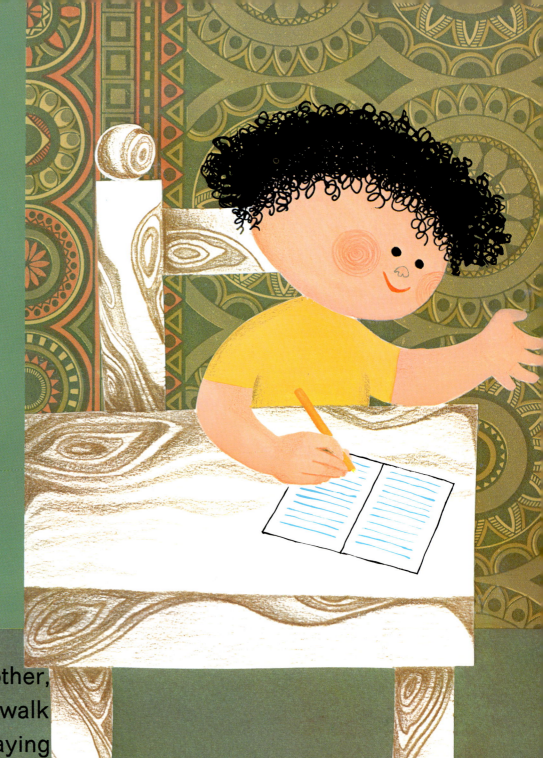

Like my baby brother,
who can't even walk
and thinks what he's saying
is just like real talk.
I love my brother.

Grownups bend down
with a creaking of knees
to ask for a hug and a kiss,
and say "Please."
I love my grownups.

If you want to say "I love you" to birds,
you have to do it without using words.

And this is the way
my dog and I say
I love you.

If she didn't love kids,
she could stay in bed late
but she's ready and waiting,
each morning at eight.
I love my teacher.

We have in our school
a real pair of twins
exactly alike,
right down to their grins.

Sometimes I wonder
how it would be
if our family could just have
another me.
My mother says,
"Thanks, I'll settle for one."
Too bad.
I think it would be loads of fun.

Not every one's happy
in our school, alas —
we have
best-friends who get mad...

And un-friends who're sad.
Well, I love them all, good kids and bad...
Because, you see, they're all my class.

Things that happen, to me, to you,
to everybody — I love them, too.
Like a rainy day.

Or a kitten display.

Or sun and sea spray.

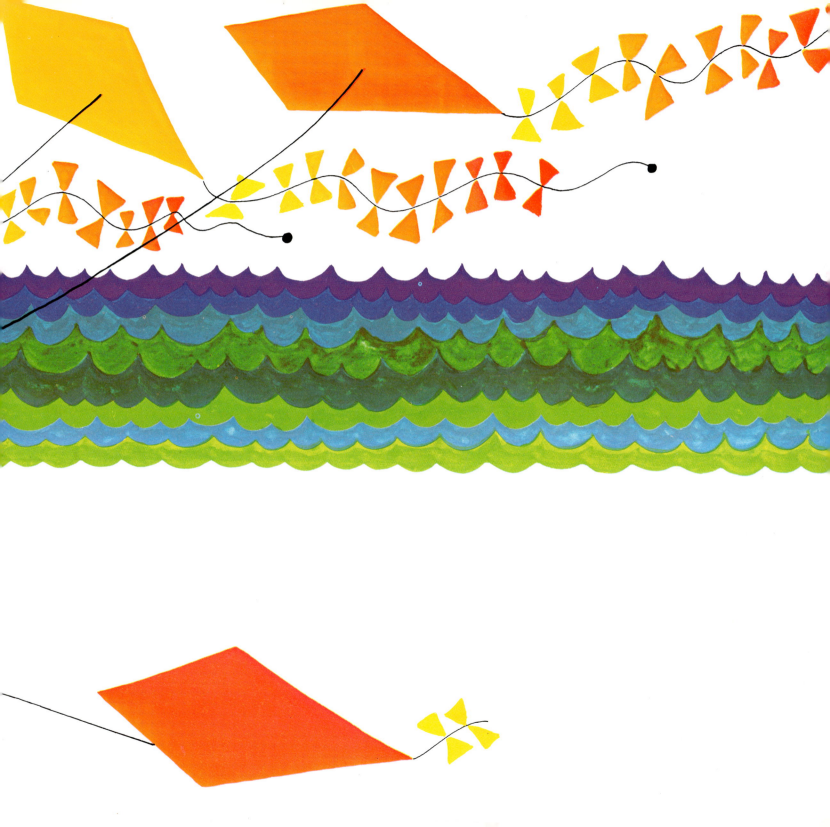

Or somebody singing in the neighborhood,
and everybody doing whatever feels good.

I
love
this.

Some things that I love
haven't happened yet:
So far,
my sister's
just preparing.

And I don't quite fit the shoes I'm wearing,
But someday I'll be a Daddy, I'll bet!

But right now, I'm tired.
I'll just close an eye,
and watch what sort of good things drift by.

For night-time can be as much fun as day.
And when I wake up,
you know what I'll say?